DIANA

Her Life in Photographs

DIANA

Her Life in Photographs

Edited by Michael O'Mara

MICHAEL O'MARA BOOKS LIMITED

First published in Great Britain in 1995 by
Michael O'Mara Books Limited
9 Lion Yard, Tremadoc Road
London SW4 7NQ

A CIP catalogue record for this book is available
from the British Library

ISBN 1-85479-749-2

Designed and typeset in Monotype Bulmer
by Martin Bristow

Printed and bound by Mohndruck, Gütersloh, Germany

10 9 8 7 6 5 4 3 2 1

Contents

Foreword

LADY DIANA SPENCER'S ARRIVAL on the 'public' scene as an apparently shy and blushing teenager in 1980 marked the beginning of the long, and not always requited, love affair between Diana and the camera. Even as a chubby-cheeked potential bride of Prince Charles, she somehow managed to shine when the cameras clicked. What's more, good photographs of Diana sent the sales of newspapers and magazines soaring. The result has been, over the years, literally millions of photographs taken by thousands of photographers for magazines from Tokyo to Topeka. As early as 1982, hardened professionals of the magazine industry were wondering how much longer the world's infatuation with Diana could last: A few months? A year? But Diana's popularity has confounded the pros; the normal rules of popularity simply do not seem to apply to her.

Why, for instance, should the people of Peru or Indonesia take such a strong interest in a Princess from a distant land when there must be local dignitaries or beauties to catch their attention?

The answer, I believe, is glamour. The Princess provides the sort of glamour that royalty of the nineteenth century or the Hollywood of the Thirties once produced. Like a Hollywood star, Diana has made her particular glamour available to the widest possible audience through the medium of photography. But no Hollywood star ever mastered the art of looking good in photographs the way the Princess has.

Interestingly, Diana's skill before the lens is not something she was born with, as the family snaps in the opening pages of this book clearly show. As a teenager, Diana was just as awkward and uncomfortable-looking while being photographed as the rest of us. It was only after her début in public life that Diana learned to lift up her eyes and look boldly into the lens. Until her recent attempts to regain her privacy, Diana gave the impression of enormous confidence before the camera – a confidence we now know (post Andrew Morton's *Diana: Her True Story*) she could not have been feeling.

Diana's sort of beauty is the kind the camera loves best. Her features are pronounced, with deep blue eyes and a magnificent set of super-white teeth. Her training in ballet helps her to carry a long and shapely frame most elegantly. No one looks better than Diana in beautiful clothing – not even models on the catwalk.

But there is a certain indefinable quality that is the key to Diana's glamour – something that makes people care about her as a person and not just an icon. She seems to have a way of making people feel they know her personally. It was certainly the case when *Diana: Her True Story* was published. There was a world-wide flood of sympathy for the Princess – the sort of sympathy most people only feel for friends and family. Whatever Diana's magic ingredient is, there is no doubt it has made her the most loved woman in the world. I hope this collection of photographs pleases Diana's many fans. I have tried to put together in one volume the very best and most important photographs of her in such a way that they would tell the story of her life. The book focuses entirely on Diana herself and does not pretend to shed any light on the ongoing drama of Britain's royal family.

MICHAEL O'MARA, 1995

1
Childhood

LEFT: *The healthy glow of country air on her cheeks, a young Diana strides out at Park House, Sandringham – the Norfolk home where she spent most of her childhood.*

BELOW: *On her first birthday, a camera-shy Diana keeps the family press at bay with a 'No pictures please' plea. Her father, the late Earl Spencer, was a keen amateur photographer.*

LEFT: *Surveying the scene from her pram – a picture taken from the family album at Park House, Sandringham. One of Diana's first memories was the smell of her plastic pram cover.*

ABOVE: *A glimpse of her spirited nature is captured by this endearing photograph of the cheeky toddler.*

ABOVE AND FACING PAGE ABOVE: *Diana's childhood was disrupted by the acrimonious divorce of her parents, the late Earl Spencer and Frances Shand-Kydd, when she was seven years old. Nonetheless, they ensured that she enjoyed many happy family holidays with her brother Charles and two sisters, Sarah and Jane. In 1970, she stayed at Itchenor, Sussex with her mother and her second husband, Peter Shand-Kydd.*

FACING PAGE BELOW: *Diana has always enjoyed a special bond with her brother Charles, who on the death of his father in March 1992, inherited the family title Earl Spencer. He now lives at Althorp House in Northampton-shire. He recently separated from his wife Victoria.*

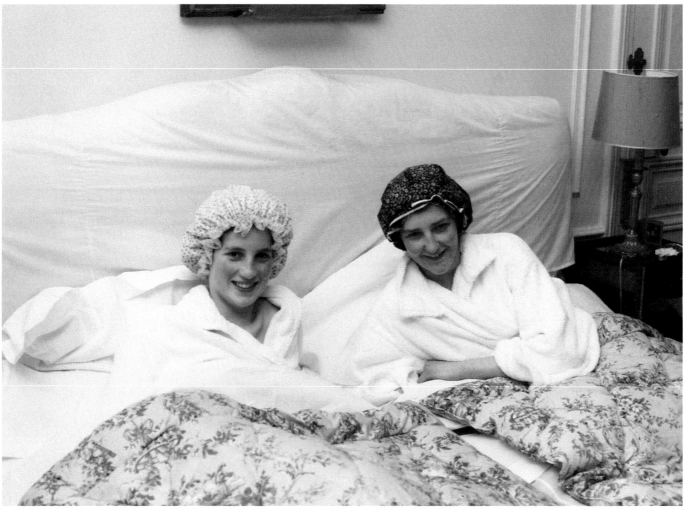

ABOVE LEFT: *The fresh-faced teenager abroad. Diana poses with her friend, Caroline Harbord-Hammond, by the banks of the river Seine in Paris, during a trip from West Heath school where she was a boarder.*

BELOW LEFT: *Relaxed and in high spirits, Diana and Caroline Harbord-Hammond clown for the camera in their bathroom attire.*

ABOVE: *A serious face on a pleasurable visit. Diana takes in the view from the top of the most famous Paris landmark, the Eiffel Tower.*

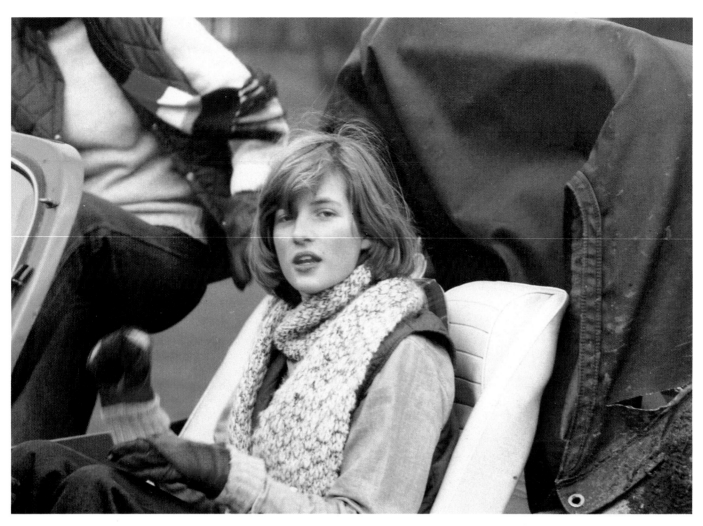

OPPOSITE ABOVE AND BELOW: *The Spencer children in a gridlock. Diana's brother Charles sits proudly at the wheel of a prized Christmas present – a blue beach buggy.*

ABOVE: *The relaxed informality of her flat-sharing days – here with Virginia Pitman – became a nostalgic dream for the young woman destined to become the Princess of Wales. Diana sits here on the roof of her Volkswagen car which she bought in 1979 and unfortunately crashed soon after.*

An athletic build enabled the streamlined Diana to win an impressive array of swimming trophies whilst a pupil at West Heath school. She even created a dive of her own – 'The Spencer Special'.

Cutting a lithe figure in her blue suit, Diana enjoyed daily swimming practice during her summer holidays. When the family moved to AlthorpHouse, her father made a priority of installing a swimming pool for his children.

Diana has always maintained her enthusiasm for swimming. She regularly swam daily at Buckingham Palace and taught her boys, William and Harry to swim at an early age.

ABOVE: *Tennis is another love of Diana's – here playing on the private courts at Althorp House. A keen member of the exclusive Chelsea Harbour Club in London, Diana plays every day. During the annual Wimbledon tournament, she is frequently spotted in the Royal Box and has been known to snatch a game with some of the more illustrious names in the game, even playing a charity doubles match with Steffi Graf.*

ABOVE RIGHT: *The late Ruth Lady Fermoy, Diana's grandmother, was an accomplished pianist who performed in front of Queen Elizabeth, the Queen Mother at the Royal Albert Hall. Her granddaughter took lessons while at school.*

BELOW RIGHT: *Diana's step-grandmother, the romantic novelist Barbara Cartland, always gave her the latest copies of her books during visits to Althorp House.*

ABOVE: *The casually-dressed teenager learned to refine her style and dress more formally for dinner and dancing when her father entertained at Althorp.*

OPPOSITE ABOVE: *Diana has always had an instinctive rapport with children. Here with Alexandra Whitaker, her first job was as a nanny to Major Jeremy and Philippa Whitaker. She worked at their Hampshire home for three months.*

OPPOSITE BELOW: *During a visit to her mother's home in Scotland, Diana kneels alongside Soufflé, her Shetland pony. After a childhood riding accident where she broke her arm, the Princess has been a reluctant horsewoman but has encouraged her sons to ride.*

ABOVE: *Exuding self-confidence, Diana leans out of her window in a face-pack and wet towel, during a school trip.*

RIGHT: *Diana strikes a balletic pose in the beautiful gardens of Althorp.*

Despite the fact that she grew to be too tall to dance professionally, Lady Diana Spencer practised her ballet routines in the gardens at Althorp. During the colder winter months, she could be found tap-dancing her way through the black and white marble entrance hall of the house.

OPPOSITE: *The bathing beauties. With her friend Mary-Ann Stewart-Richardson, Diana sits beside one of her favourite places, the pool at Althorp House.*

LEFT: *Diana, her brother Charles and friend Mary-Ann Stewart-Richardson, relax in front of the television. These days the Princess keeps up with the long-running soap operas which gives her a useful topic for conversation when she meets the public.*

BELOW: *Her sister Sarah's legs draped over her shoulders, Diana enjoys an evening's fun with her family at Althorp.*

LEFT: *A snap of a card-game. Diana plays her hand against friend Alexandra Loyd. She was taught card games by her late grandmother, Ruth Lady Fermoy.*

BELOW: *Diana visits her brother Charles at Maidwell preparatory school, where he was a boarder.*

RIGHT: *Her right foot curled in, the embarrassment shows as a timid Diana hides behind her bobbed haircut. It is an early indication of the 'Shy Di' look which enchanted the world.*

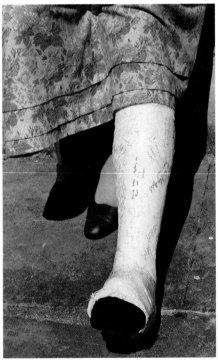

LEFT AND ABOVE: *A disastrous skiing trip left Diana's left leg encased in a plaster cast for several months. Friends and family wrote witty and sympathetic messages to Diana over the cast including Simon Berry who scribbled, 'You've been skating on thin ice lately.'*

RIGHT: *Displaying the typical nerves of a young girl, Diana poses for a photograph at Althorp House but is an unwilling model.*

LEFT: *The Spencer girls. Diana sits back-to-back with her elder sister Jane – someone she respects enormously and has often turned to for advice.*

TOP: *Today, one of Diana's crowning glories is her trademark short blonde highlighted hair. When younger, her hair was light brown.*

ABOVE: *With his much-prized trophy in his arms, cricketer James Cain carries Diana from the field after winning the match. Diana and her friends enjoyed attending the friendly encounters between the local village team and Althorp House.*

ABOVE LEFT: *Diana takes an upside-down look at the world, while reclining on a sofa bed. She had joined a chalet party for a skiing holiday organized by her friend Simon Berry.*

BELOW LEFT: *Brotherly love from Charles. This photograph was taken by their father.*

BELOW: *Few could be immune to the attractions of Lady Diana Spencer. Certainly, Humphrey Butler, who later became an auctioneer at Christie's, looks content to have her on his knee.*

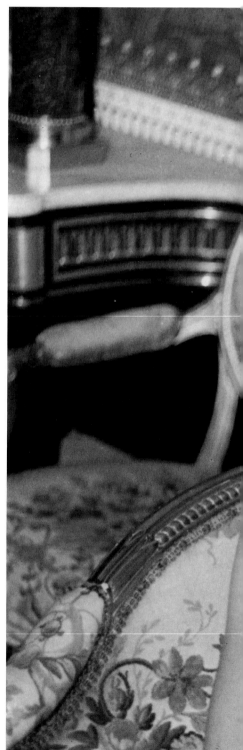

Amidst the splendour of the stately Althorp House, Diana adds her own touch of glamour
with what has now become one of her trademarks – pearls. A hint of cleavage on show,
the maturing Lady Diana Spencer poses for her father in a low-cut evening dress,
in the hallway of Althorp House before a ball in 1980.

LEFT: *In the days leading up to her wedding, Diana's hesitant glance expressed her youth and innocence, her eyes betraying the unworldliness of a girl not yet turned twenty.*

RIGHT: *Walking in Cowdray Park, Diana enjoys a chat with Sarah Ferguson, who later became her sister-in-law, the Duchess of York.*

ABOVE: *Diana at the Young England kindergarten school in Pimlico, London. This was taken in 1980 when press interest in her became intense.*

RIGHT: *Sunlight streams through Diana's flimsy summer dress, famously showing her long legs to the world. The young kindergarten teacher who had innocently posed for the photograph was mortified.*

LEFT: *Now officially engaged, Diana started to dress the part. Photographers went wild when she appeared in this daring off-the-shoulder black ballgown, worn to a charity recital at Goldsmith's Hall in London in March 1981.*

RIGHT: *Diana cuts a dash at a polo match in Windsor Park with a distinctive sheep motif jumper and red shoes. Already Diana's fashion style was in evidence.*

2
Princess

LEFT: *In a classic regal portrait, the Princess of Wales poses for photographer Lord Snowdon in 1985, effortlessly demonstrating her natural elegance and poise.*

BELOW: *Diana looks every inch the happy young mother in this official study by Tim Graham, taken only a few months after the birth of Prince William.*

ABOVE: *The early pictures of Diana show a marked difference in her facial features. In this intimate portrait by Lord Snowdon, he captures her healthy glow and plump cheeks – in contrast to later pictures where a hollow look – due to extreme weight loss – had left her gaunt and pale. Diana's battle with the slimmer's disease, bulimia, has now been well recorded and she has since spoken openly of the problems of addiction.*

RIGHT: *Patrick Lichfield took the official portraits of Diana on her wedding day on 29 July 1981. The ceremony was broadcast to 600 million people around the world.*

LEFT: *From the start, there has never been a shortage of crowds to see the Princess of Wales. Here a drenched Diana fulfils her first duties as a royal wife with a walkabout in Carmarthen, Wales. She has since recalled, 'The people who stood outside for hours and hours in the torrential rain. They were so welcoming . . . I was terrified.'*

ABOVE: *The plumpness of her bachelor days is gone. Here, having already shed several pounds since her engagement, a sylph-like Diana bares her shoulders at an official function at the Victoria and Albert Museum, London, in 1981.*

LEFT: *In 1982, just three months before the birth of Prince William, the mother-to-be radiates happiness and good health at a function at the Barbican, London.*

RIGHT: *A few months after William's birth the effects of the slimmer's disease, bulimia, were all too apparent when Diana attended the premiere of* E.T.

ABOVE: *Since her entry into the royal family, Diana has inherited and been presented with priceless jewelry, much of it given by the Queen. Here, just a year after her marriage, her youthful looks are enhanced to a more sophisticated elegance with the addition of diamonds and pearls.*

RIGHT: *Mother and son. Diana proudly shows off baby Prince William to Tim Graham's camera at Kensington Palace.*

*Diana's charm and natural beauty
were perfectly suited to the informal
atmosphere of life in Australia.
In 1983 she drew admiring glances
during an official tour and is
pictured here in Sydney (left) and
looking soulful at Ayers Rock (right).*

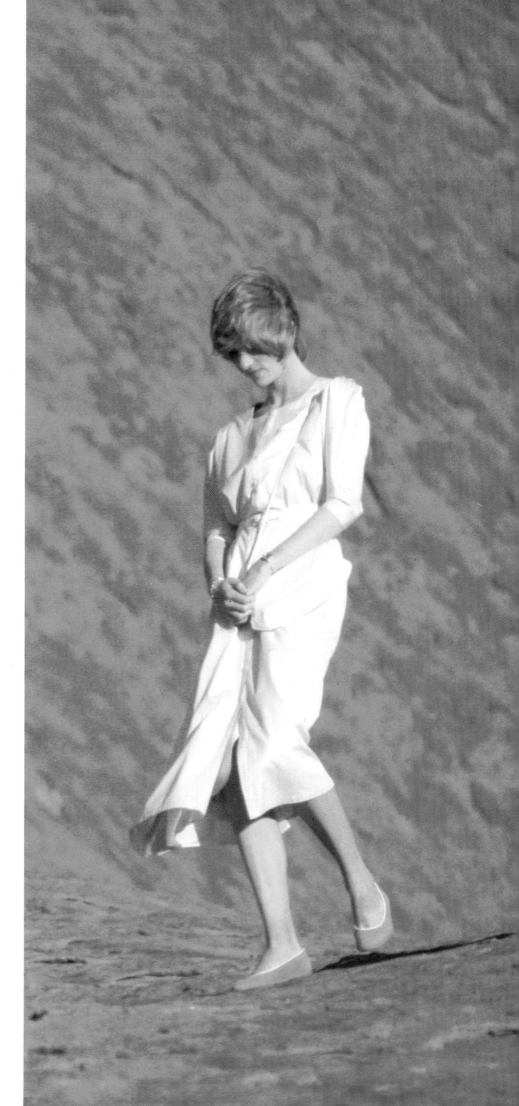

LEFT: *Thrilling the crowds has always been Diana's forte. She has the knack of putting people at their ease with her good humour and attention to detail. Here she responds to the electric atmosphere of well-wishers in Masterton, New Zealand.*

ABOVE: *Motherhood certainly agreed with the royal wife. Glowing with happiness, she appeared to be perfectly suited to her new royal life.*

LEFT: *The Australian Prime Minister, Malcolm Fraser encouraged Diana to bring baby William along on the 1983 tour, which meant that the royal couple were able to extend their tour by an extra two weeks to include New Zealand. Here Diana is pictured in Auckland.*

ABOVE: *Diana has always managed to combine the purity of her youthful looks with the stunning sensuality of a sophisticated woman. She keeps her make-up light and simple, allowing the richness of her jewels to add an almost ethereal look to this regal portrait.*

LEFT: *While on a royal tour of Canada, Diana celebrated her twenty-second birthday.*
Never short of admirers, she clutches an armful of floral gifts during a visit to Edmonton.

ABOVE: *It was certainly a feather in Diana's cap to inspect the line-up of the Royal Newfoundland*
Constabulary during the tour of Canada in 1983. By now, her universal appeal was unquestioned.
'The Princess of Wales has done more to popularize the concept of monarchy throughout the world
than any other member of the Royal Family in the last ten years', noted one authority.

ABOVE: *Setting the right tone with her choice of outfits has never been a problem for the fashion-conscious Princess. During a tour of Canada, she highlighted her youthful beauty by sticking to simple, classical designs.*

RIGHT: *The Princess has never been a fan of polo, but her dazzling presence enlightened many a dull match. Here, she stands hands-on-hips at a match in Cirencester. Not a keen horsewoman herself, she has even commented to friends that, 'In another incarnation the last thing I would ever want to be is a horse.'*

LEFT: *The formal elegance of red, suits the blonde hair and blue eyes of the Princess of Wales. Shimmering in sequins and lace during a visit to Norway, she holds the camera in thrall.*

RIGHT: *Pregnant with her second child, Harry, this period of Diana's life in 1984 was one of her happiest. She had by this stage discovered from a scan that her unborn child was to be another boy.*

*In 1984, Diana sported a longer, softer hairstyle. Here she
is seen visiting Dr. Barnardos in the East End of London.*

*Diana in Southampton – as ever, perfectly groomed for
her public duties.*

Two portraits of a modern Princess.
Delightful, fresh-faced informality (above) and dazzling,
classical regal beauty (right).

ABOVE: *The perfect English Rose.*

RIGHT: *Diana claimed on this visit to Italy in 1985 that, 'My clothes were far from my mind.' This is difficult to believe of the Princess, whose choice of attire for foreign visits has always been subtly blended with her surroundings. Here, her striking outfit was the ideal choice for a visit to the naval base at La Spezia.*

In October 1985, Diana fulfilled her role as Colonel-in-Chief of the Royal Hampshire Regiment, based in West Berlin. After inspecting the troops, she gamely donned a tracksuit and hopped into a 15-ton tank for a driving lesson.

LEFT: *Her caring nature has drawn Diana into the lives of many less fortunate and privileged people. From the homeless and mentally ill, to Aids sufferers, she has managed to reach out and embrace a huge range of needy causes. Here she flashes one of her famously therapeutic smiles for the patients at St. Joseph's Hospice in London.*

ABOVE AND BELOW: *The role she has always said she loves best – motherhood. In these two photographs taken by Tim Graham at Kensington Palace, she helps William with a jigsaw (above) and shows the two boys how to form a double act on the piano (below).*

ABOVE: *A surprise party for royal valet Ken Stronach on board the flight to Australia in 1985, brought Diana from her private quarters to join in the celebrations with her staff.*

RIGHT: *Arriving in Melbourne, Diana is in a jovial mood before disembarkation.*

LEFT: *Diana is besieged with flowers as she kneels and talks to children from Macedon, Victoria. In 1983, severe bush fires devastated the area, killing more than one hundred people.*

ABOVE: *'She would even look good in a sack', observed Princess Michael of Kent, her next door neighbour at Kensington Palace.*

THIS PAGE: *A royal visit to the USA in 1985 finds Diana in a more sombre, formal mood. At Arlington Cemetery (above) and at a function in Washington (right).*

FAR RIGHT: *When Diana attended a dinner given in honour of the royal couple by the British Ambassador and his wife in Washington, the Princess topped her beautiful, cream evening gown with this pearl and diamond tiara, a wedding gift from the Queen.*

LEFT: *Even just a glimpse of the smiling Princess through a rain-spattered window, has brought much joy to her adoring public.*

RIGHT: *Towering over her hosts, the statuesque Princess of Wales slips into a beautiful kimono, a gift from the Kimono-Makers Association in Kyoto, during a visit to Japan in 1986.*

LEFT AND ABOVE: *In the days before her separation, the Princess of Wales kept a busy diary that needed expert co-ordination and consultation. In her private sitting room at Kensington Palace, she conducts her business meetings with her current private secretary, Patrick Jephson.*

BELOW: *Designers Elizabeth and David Emanuel found favour with Diana after creating her wedding dress in 1981. They would bring fabrics and sketches to her apartment for approval. Nowadays she is more likely to visit the designer showrooms herself.*

LEFT: *At Highgrove, William and Harry have been able to enjoy the beautiful countryside and keep pets of their own. Smokey the Shetland pony was an ideal choice to initiate the young princes into the sport of riding.*

———

RIGHT: *Diana takes Prince Harry to face Tim Graham's camera in his special paratrooper's outfit.*

RIGHT: *A playful pose on the doorstep at Highgrove.*

BELOW: *Diana's pride and joy – William and Harry. Harry especially is keen on the army. His room at Kensington Palace is adorned with numerous military pictures.*

LEFT: *The desert Princess pictured in Oman in 1986,
during a tour of the Gulf States.*

ABOVE: *'To be modern, yet keep the mystique – that is
the trick', noted one observer. Diana has always been
adept at mastering the two.*

Diana's life has never been plain-sailing but it has certainly presented her with exceptional challenges and excitements. Even here, preparing to fly around the Highgrove estate by helicopter, she has enjoyed a tremendously privileged view of life.

Both Diana and her sister-in-law, Sarah, Duchess of York, are keen skiers. Before they separated from their respective husbands, their friendship was especially close and Sarah's high spirits encouraged Diana to drop her formal guard on occasion. In 1987 they descended the slopes together in Klosters and clowned before the cameras.

LEFT: *Diana puts William in a spin.*

ABOVE AND RIGHT: *Diana and her two boys lend their support at polo matches, although Diana is not keen on horses herself.*

LEFT: 'In the nicest possible way, she is well aware that she is a dish', said author Clive James. With her model looks and unique sense of style, Diana is the most admired and fashionable member of the royal family since Queen Alexandra.

ABOVE: Diana's make-up style has remained resolutely unchanged over the years. One of her best features are her eyes which are cornflower blue and are emphasized by bright blue eyeliner. On her lips she tends to opt for natural reds and pinks, lightly glossed over.

LEFT: *Getting used to the cameras has been made easier for the young princes after taking part in official photo calls, such as this one in Spain, where more than 60 lenses were pointed in their direction.*

RIGHT: *Three years and one day old, Prince Harry meets his new headteacher, Miss Mynor, who ran the Wetherby school in Kensington.*

LEFT: *Diana has travelled much of the world since acquiring her royal status. Here she contemplates the majestic sights of the Temple of the Emerald Buddha, in Bangkok, Thailand.*

RIGHT: *Diana, who is 5-feet-10-inches tall, mostly opts for sensibly low-heeled shoes so as not to tower over those she meets. This line-up of Australian lifeguards still manage to look almost diminutive by her side.*

LEFT: *Diana's electric presence can sometimes put others
in the shade.*

ABOVE: *Viewing the sights, Thai-style, in Bangkok.*

LEFT: *A devoted mother, it has long been known that Diana yearned to have a little girl to complete her family. Here she watches Trooping the Colour with Lady Rose and Lady Davina Windsor.*

BELOW LEFT AND RIGHT: *The appearance of the Princess at polo matches gave rise to informal duties – presenting the prizes.*

RIGHT: *'Her off-duty style could be characterized as sensual masculinity',* observed royal author *Andrew Morton.*

LEFT: *Always supportive of British designers, Diana pays Bruce Oldfield the ultimate compliment of turning out for this Barnardos gala evening in a stunning mauve, off-the-shoulder, velvet gown. It was created by the designer, himself a former Barnardos boy.*

RIGHT: *Cool in blue, the Princess of Wales and the Duchess of York cut a dash as they leave Sandringham church in Norfolk.*

Dressing for the evening is when Diana's true beauty is really allowed to shine. Her tall, slim figure perfectly suits the intricate and sophisticated gowns she chooses to wear and she is imaginative and bold when it comes to her choice of jewelry. She often opts for fakes and has been known to alter family heirlooms.

LEFT: *Attending the Arc de Triomphe Armistice Commemoration in Paris in November 1989.*

BELOW AND RIGHT: *'Shy Di' she may have been in her early days, but once the confidence came, Diana knew how to make the most of her assets. 'The Princess of Wales knows that if clothes are going to talk, less says more', noted one fashion critic.*

*Supporting her children at their school events has always
been a priority in the Princess's diary. Nimble of foot, she
wins the Mother's Day race in 1989 at William's sports
day. Diana was thrilled: 'This is the first time in my life
I've ever won anything like this', she commented.*

Relaxing in the sun with William at a game of polo at
Windsor Great Park.

Patrick Demarchelier is one of Diana's favourite photographers and these pictures were commissioned from him by British VOGUE *in 1990. He brilliantly captures both the exquisite young mother (left) and the glorious beauty of the Princess (above).*

Today, the intrusive cameras that follow Diana's every move are no longer willingly tolerated. On holiday, she can never escape the prying photographers who often go to absurd lengths to get an exclusive. Even a bike ride in the Scilly Isles (right) isn't sacred for the holidaying mum.

LEFT: *Diana observes the customs of the foreign countries she visits and during this tour of Kuwait in 1989, she obeyed the Islamic dictate of covering hair, shoulders and knees in public.*

RIGHT: *In Dubai, the blue turban-style hat encapsulates a sense of Arabia.*

A keep-fit enthusiast, Diana enjoyed the national launch of 'Bike '89' on 18 April in aid of the British Lung Foundation. Making the excuse that her skirt was too tight, she politely turned down the offer of riding one of the bicycles around the park.

―――――

A thoroughly modern mum doing the school run. Diana has a penchant for American clothing – baseball caps and cowboy boots.

RIGHT AND BELOW: *The Princess of Wales with her mother, Mrs. Frances Shand-Kydd, attend the wedding of Diana's brother, Charles to former model, Victoria Lockwood at Great Brington, near Althorp on 16 September 1990.*

FACING PAGE: *In Indonesia, Diana finds time for a quick game of bowls in front of an impressed gathering. She was visiting the Sitanala leprosy hospital on the outskirts of Jakarta.*

LEFT: *In a dazzling, beaded evening gown, Diana shimmers in her full glory at the opening ceremony for the new Hong Kong Cultural Centre on her trip to the Far East. She has been a recipient of many generous gifts of jewelry and antiques over the years and here she wears a pearl and diamond bracelet, given to her by a friend.*

RIGHT: *In Lagos, she chose a beautiful, white chiffon dress, picked out with violet flowers and green leaves, for an official function.*

LEFT: *A little crumpled in the African heat, Diana may have met her match amongst the exotic array of tribal costumes surrounding her. 'The things I do for England', she often jokes with friends, as she regales them with tales of her foreign trips.*

RIGHT: *During her visit to Nigeria in 1990, the President's wife, Mrs. Babangida, took Diana under her wing. During a ceremony, the delighted Princess received gifts from local women.*

ABOVE: *When Diana was photographed during a family holiday on the Caribbean island of Necker wearing animal-print beachwear, it instantly became a hit with all fashion-conscious women.*

RIGHT: *Her boys growing up, Diana still takes pride in doing the school trips whenever she can. Here, she takes William and Harry back for the beginning of the summer term at their preparatory school in Kensington.*

LEFT: *Film and theatre events are a great excuse to make a grand entrance. On 5 June 1990, Diana stunned onlookers in satin and lace for a charity gala evening at Sadler's Wells Theatre in London.*

RIGHT *'She is genuinely beautiful. I don't know why she needs me really', her make-up artist Barbara Daly once said.*

LEFT AND RIGHT: *Thank goodness for a sense of humour. Whatever her personal problems, Diana has kept on smiling. She knows that the public do not want to see a glum Princess.*

OVERLEAF: *Flanked by her sons, Diana heads for the mountains. Although she enjoys skiing, the tragedy in Klosters when one of their group was killed in an avalanche, left Diana understandably shaken for some time. Since her separation, she often skis with friends.*

Come rain or shine, Diana always looks beautiful and manages to make the most of every situation, even when the elements are against her.

ABOVE LEFT: *At the premiere of* Stepping Out, *Diana and film star Liza Minnelli share an intimate chat. For a time they became close friends and shared many trans-atlantic telephone conversations.*

BELOW LEFT: *A starry line-up where even Hollywood's biggest names want to meet the world's most famous royal.*

RIGHT: *Dazzling in the dark, Diana dresses in pearls and velvet in January 1992, for the Hong Kong Gala evening at the Barbican in London.*

LEFT: *A face of serenity. The Princess of Wales is lost in her private thoughts during a trip to Cairo.*

RIGHT: *Baseball cap, shorts and sneakers have always marked Diana out as an informal parent. She tries to lead as normal a life as possible when off duty, particularly when she is with her children.*

ABOVE: *On the Caribbean island of Nevis, Diana, the two boys and their friends have fun diving from their boat.*

RIGHT: *Diana enjoys shopping, particularly for her boys. Here in Cirencester, she has often been spotted popping into sweet and toy shops, stocking up with goodies.*

147

3
Princess Alone

LEFT: *A battery of photographers were present when the Princess attended the Headway charity event at the Hilton Hotel in December 1993. During the event, she delivered her 'resignation speech' when she appealed for herself and her children to be given 'time and space.'*

BELOW: *Despite her plea, Diana will always remain hot property for the world's press and her lone sorties through the streets of London still provide newsworthy coverage. Going from being the most famous royal in the world to being a free spirit without proper guard caused major headaches for the police.*

ABOVE: *Diana enjoys the surf with her boys.*

RIGHT: *Slowly, Diana has begun accepting more public duties again, albeit at a much reduced level. Here she attends the ISDD Media Awards lunch in London where she was presented with a special award for her successful work concerning the misuse of drugs.*

Determined to counteract the stuffiness of the Palace,
Diana continues to take her sons and their friends to
public attractions like leisure parks and fast-food bars.

*Preferring now to be left alone by the paparazzi, Diana is
more likely to be hiding behind dark glasses or running in
the opposite direction when approached by photographers
in the street.*

LEFT: *Diana in a swimsuit shows off her statuesque figure at its best. Daily work-outs and a good diet help her to keep her enviable figure.*

ABOVE: *Holidays spent at the playgrounds of the rich have attracted Diana since she has been on her own. Whether with her sons or in the company of friends, she makes sure she jets off to sunnier climes whenever she has the chance.*

LEFT: *At the New York fashion awards in 1995, Diana tried out a new look with a slicked-back hairstyle. The reactions were not altogether favourable.*

RIGHT: *Looking tanned and happy, Diana enjoys a vacation on St. Barthélemy in the Caribbean, February 1995.*

Picture Acknowledgments

Press Association: 8, 9, 10, 11, 12, 13, 23 (*bottom*)

The Late Earl Spencer's Family Album: 14, 15, 16, 17, 18, 19, 20, 21, 22, 23 (*top*), 24, 25, 26, 27, 28, 29, 30, 31, 32, 33, 34, 35, 36, 37, 38, 39

Tim Graham Picture Library: 1, 40, 41, 42, 47, 50, 51, 53, 54, 55, 56, 57, 58, 59, 60, 61, 62, 63, 64, 65, 66, 68, 69, 70, 71, 72, 73, 74, 75, 76, 77, 78, 79, 80, 81, 82, 83, 84, 85, 86, 87, 88, 89, 90, 91, 92, 93, 94, 95, 96, 99, 100, 101, 102, 103, 104, 105, 107, 108, 109, 110, 111, 112, 113, 114, 115, 116 (*top and bottom*), 117, 120, 121, 122, 123, 124, 125, 126 (*top*), 127, 128, 129, 130, 131, 132, 133, 134, 135, 136, 138, 139, 140, 141, 142 (*bottom*), 143, 144, 151, 156, 157, 159

Rex Features: 43, Scarlett Dyer

Camera Press: 2, 118, 119, Patrick Demarchelier; 44, 45, Tony Drabble; 46, 48, Snowdon; 49, Patrick Lichfield; 52, Joe Bulaitis; 126 (*bottom*), Mike Anthony; 150, Tom Wargacki

Alpha: 67, 98, Jim Bennett; 97, 106, 158, Alpha; 116 (*centre*), 145, 146, 148, 152, 153, Dave Chancellor; 137, Tim Anderson; 142 (*top*), Dave Bennett; 147, C. Postlethwaite

The Glenn Harvey Picture Collection: 149, 155

The following pictures attributed to *Tim Graham Picture Library* were not taken by Tim Graham nor were they supplied by either him or anyone connected with him: 42, 116 (*top and bottom*), 120, 121, 156, 157, 159